Betty Pfeiffer took her first steps in realizing the wonders of the ocean's creatures while scuba diving. The dive master handed her asea cucumber. He then brought forth a baby octopus about eighteen inches long to touch. She still remembers the silky feel of the octopus beneath her hand and the gentle wrap of its tentacles around her arm. Betty took that encounter and continued her journey of learning about ocean life. In her new book, *The Beauties and The Beasts*, she now offers others some of the amazing things she has discovered.

THE Beauties AND THE Beasts

CREATURES AT THE BOTTOM OF THE OCEAN

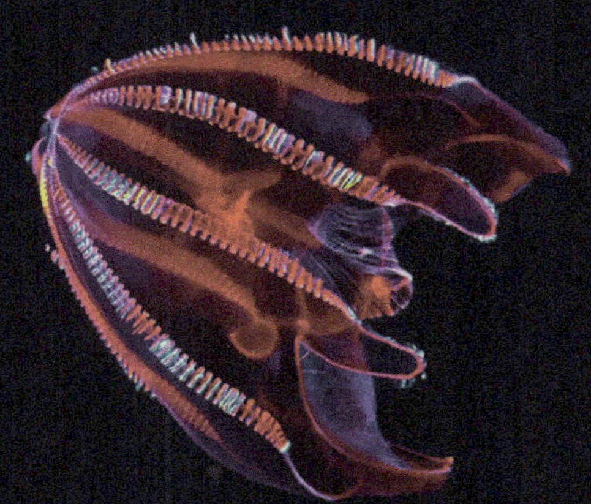

BETTY PFEIFFER

AUSTIN MACAULEY PUBLISHERS™

LONDON * CAMBRIDGE * NEW YORK * SHARJAH

Ordering Information

Quantity sales: Special discounts are available on quantity purchases by corporations, associations, and others. For details, contact the publisher at the address below.

Publisher's Cataloging-in-Publication data

Pfeiffer, Betty

The Beauties and The Beasts

ISBN 9798886933048 (Paperback)

ISBN 9781685627959 (Hardback)

ISBN 9798886933055 (ePub e-book)

Library of Congress Control Number: 2023924418

www.austinmacauley.com/us

First Published 2024

Austin Macauley Publishers LLC

40 Wall Street, 33rd Floor, Suite 3302

New York, NY 10005

USA

mail-usa@austinmacauley.com

+1 (646) 5125767

This book is dedicated to my husband Richard Pfeiffer who was always and ever my biggest fan and my toughest critic.

The Beauties and The Beasts would not have been possible without the delightful suggestions, welcomed criticisms, and needed support of my good writer friends. They kept me on the right track when so much about the ocean fascinated me.

There's nothing wrong with enjoying looking at the surface of the ocean itself, except that when you finally see what goes on underwater, you realize that you've been missing the whole point of the ocean. Staying on the surface all the time is like going to the circus and staring at the outside of the tent.
Dave Barry, American author and columnist.

At the Bottom of the Ocean

We're about to take a dive through a place of *almost* to *absolute* darkness—so deep in the ocean the sun can't begin to penetrate the water to give even a glimpse of light.

But stranger than the lack of sunlight are the creatures that call this blackout home. They have learned to thrive under pressure that would turn most life to mush, cold just next to freezing, or temperatures so hot they would turn a hamburger to ash. And with the vastness of the ocean for their home, many of these strange beings choose to stay in one place for their entire life. They like it where they are. That's not only strange—it's weird! So are they.

Are you prepared to meet the cute and the curious creatures hanging out at the bottom of the ocean? Beautiful? Ugly? Fierce? Freaky? How about from microscopic to mammoth?

If you think you're ready, let's go.

Take a deep breath. Imagine you are in one of the **submersibles,** carefully fashioned to withstand more pressure than our military submarines can handle. Without protection, like James Cameron had when he descended almost seven miles to the bottom of the Challenger Deep, you'd turn into a gob of goo before you knew it.

Why? Because our bodies are fine-tuned to exist in a certain amount of air pressure. You notice the difference in your ears when you go up a mountain.

Challenger Deep

The Challenger Deep is a trench at the bottom of the Pacific Ocean near the island of Guam. Ocean trenches are usually long with steep sides. They are not very wide but very deep, and Challenger Deep is the deepest of the deep anywhere on this world. It has a recorded depth of 35,876 feet (10,935 meters). That's

almost 6.8 miles below the surface of the ocean.

You probably would say, "My ears are popping!" Well, they really aren't popping. Your body is adjusting to the difference in the air pressure you are used to living in and the lesser air pressure you find yourself in as you ascend.

Down there, where the dark seems thick enough to slice, the pressure is like having 250 cars piled on your head. We aren't designed to withstand the enormous pressure change of *this* trip.

To make our journey, we'll need a high-tech craft. There are many to choose from, but Human Occupied Vehicle (HOV), Alvin, can carry passengers and get to about 98 percent of the ocean floor, reaching a depth of 21,325 feet (6,500 meters). **Certification** for this depth was awarded in 2022.

There is a large titanium sphere inside Alvin's twenty-three feet long and eleven-and-a-half feet high outer casing—about the size of an average travel trailer. In the sphere, up in front over the **manipulator arms** and sample baskets, sit the pilot and one or two scientists. That's where you and I will be as we spy on some of the creatures inhabiting the darkest of the dark.

We'll have five viewports to give us overlapping sight—almost a **panoramic** view. The ability to see where we are going is essential. It is hard to make plans in advance because the pilot and scientists know so little about the bottom of the ocean. We'll just have to get down there, look around, and explore where instincts and present knowledge take us.

So let's put Alvin to the test.

We're passing through the **Sunlight Zone,** where the light of the sun can penetrate the water. Now we're at 656 feet (200 meters), where we begin our descent through the **Twilight Zone.** Take off your sunglasses. Even at the top of the Twilight Zone, not enough sunlight enters to permit **photosynthesis** to occur. This part of our trip lasts until we reach 3,280 feet (1,000 meters), gradually becoming darker and darker.

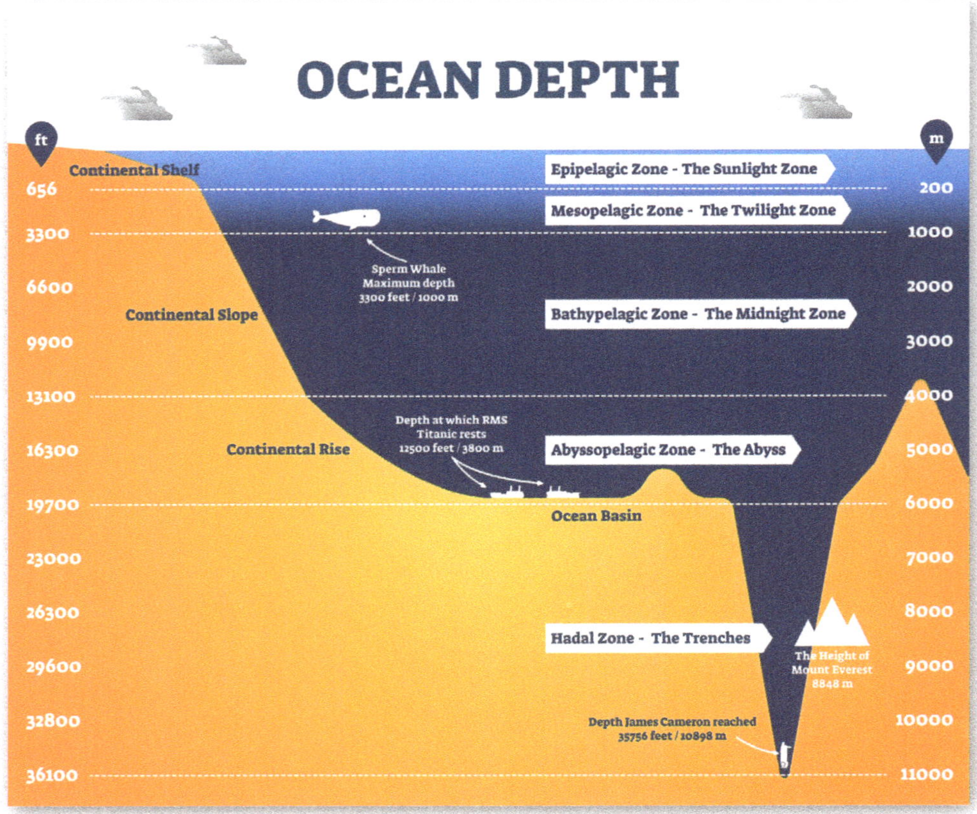

We probably won't realize when we slip from the Twilight Zone into the **Midnight Zone**. The absence of light is astonishing. Midnight up on land can't begin to give you an idea of how dark the ocean at this depth can be.

The word "photic" means a particle of light or photon. The technical name for the Midnight Zone is aphotic—*without a particle* of light. We'll definitely need Alvin's bright beams if we want to see very much down here. Still, many of the creatures make their own light with **bioluminescence**. Watch for them.

Bioluminescence

Light cannot penetrate below 656 feet (200 meters). Creatures in the twilight zone and below make their own light with bioluminescence through a chemical reaction. The one essential chemical for it to work is luciferin. When luciferin combines with luciferase or oxygen, it produces light.

As blue travels through water most easily, it is the one most often seen. The shrimp in this photo has special glands that make it able to 'vomit' blue light.

However, deep-sea creatures can also produce many colors along the spectrum, from almost lavender to yellows and greens. Occasionally some species will be able to make red light, although it is rare. Different species use different chemicals to manufacture their light.

Bioluminescence in the deep, dark ocean has a variety of uses. These light displays can attract prey, confuse predators, and communicate. The scarce red light is used by some as a searchlight. Most fish in the deep ocean can't see red, so the one with the red searchlight can swim right up to its prey without being seen.

NOAA believes perhaps 90 percent of the ocean's creatures in the Midnight Zone and the lower part of the Twilight Zone, below 1,640 feet, are bioluminescent. When bacteria live inside other animals, they can luminesce and create light for the animal they are living in.

There—a spout of white coming from a **hydrothermal vent**. Do you see it? It looks like the smokestack of a manufacturing plant, but this spout is not smoke or steam. This white plume is ice-cold seawater that seeped into cracks in the bottom of the ocean and got hot—really hot! Sometimes it will get up to 750° F (399° C). The heated water draws in chemicals and minerals from the super-heated rocks. This hot mixture of chemicals, unimaginably, becomes the life-fueling energy for **microbes**, which themselves become food for other creatures.

Extremophiles

Remember, there is no sunlight down here, so photosynthesis is not possible. How, then, do microbes, bacteria, and even larger creatures get food? These unbelievably adaptive **extremophiles** do it through a process called **chemosynthesis**.

Rising in both white plumes and those called "black smokers" is a witch's brew of chemicals. Microbes and bacteria lap up what they like and convert the chemicals into energy.

This *chemosynthesis* is similar to how plants, receiving the sun's rays, create energy or food through *photosynthesis.*

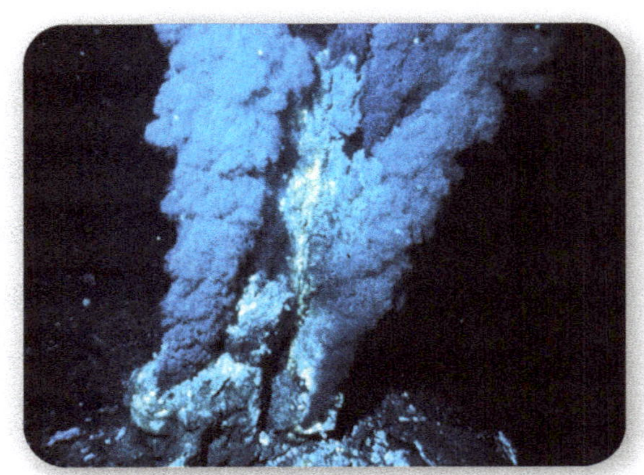

Hydrothermal vents

Perhaps you've noticed a pipe coming from the roofs of houses. That is a plumbing vent connected to the drain system of the house. Why is it there? It lets sewer gases and odors escape, and permits air to enter the drainpipe. When air can get into the drainpipe, it prevents the creation of a negative air pressure.

Hydrothermal vents act in much the same way, permitting chemicals, minerals, and heat to travel up from inside the earth. The island of Cyprus is famous for its enormous copper resources that were formed over the ages by hydrothermal vents. At some point, the earth gave a heave and lifted the vent system up high enough to become dry land.

The desire for clean energy increases the need for minerals such as cobalt, graphite, lithium, and manganese, but the quantities we are able to mine are diminishing. Some are seriously looking at the prospect of mining the ocean floor. There are pros and cons to this idea. Can you think what they might be?

Extremophiles

If you've ever said, "I can't stand this," you most likely meant something was uncomfortable for you. You didn't like it, but you really wouldn't die from it.

Extremophiles can live in conditions that would kill us. So why don't they die? Some of them actually love their extreme home. They are called 'extremophilic'. (Think of Philadelphia, the city of brotherly love. Here the suffix 'philic' means those organisms love where they are.) They thrive on extreme heat, pressure, and lack of oxygen. It seems whatever life at the vents at the bottom of the ocean can throw at them, they thoroughly enjoy.

Others, the extremotolerant organisms, are better off in somewhat more ordinary (for us) conditions. They have adapted and can survive one or more of the extreme conditions.

Let's meet some of these creatures who seem to love a nasty chemical soup, extreme temperatures of hot and cold, and extreme pressure sufficient to make a navy submarine implode. They deserve the name "extremophiles."

The following conversations with the deep-sea creatures are (of course) imagined. However, all the information is real and true, even though one or two may seem impossible.

The "Ugly Award"

"I am a blob—well, a blobfish. Thank you for your smile—not all humans have that reaction. The scientists on the Research Vessel Tangaroa affectionately named me Mr. Blobby. Did you know I won an award? In 2013, I was voted the ugliest animal alive.

"However, I am quite happy

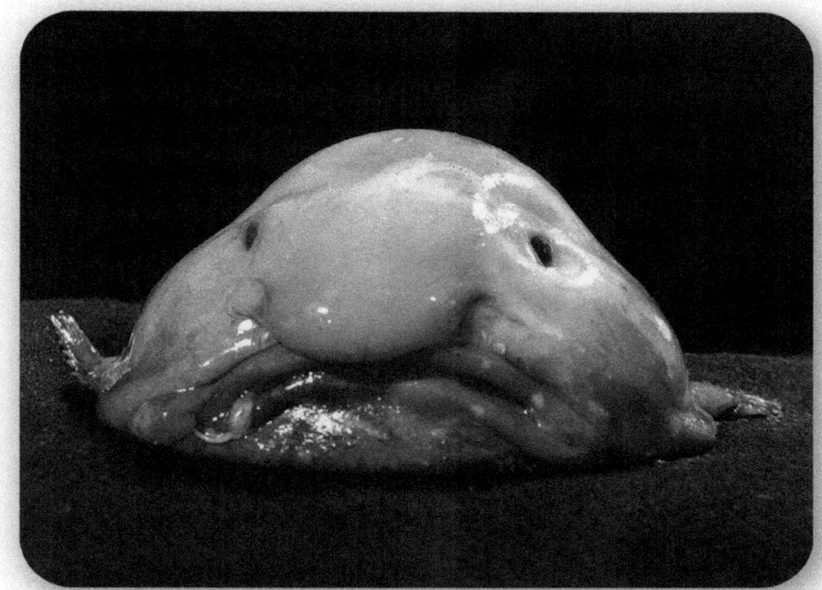

This is how a blobfish looks when brought up out of the water.

in my skin. After all, it's pretty much all I have—no bones and no swim bladder. Because I prefer the deeper parts of the ocean, there's a lot of pressure put on one small fish down here. It would smash me to pieces if I had the bones and swim bladder of those less adventurous fish that stay up in the lighter, brighter zones. I simply use my very supple—well, mooshy—body to let me float a little above the bottom of the ocean.

"Some say I'm overweight because I'm only about twelve inches long and weigh maybe twenty pounds. I guess compared to a loaf of bread, which is about my size but weighs less than two pounds, it might seem heavy. I've just never found it a problem.

A blobfish under water looks like any other fish.

"If you'd come down to 3,000 or 4,000 feet (900 or 1200 meters) deep in the ocean with me, you would see I look a lot like other fish. The pressure is my friend and shapes me up pretty well. For you humans, not so much. Only when you insist on dragging me up to your level do you tend to use terms like **"gelatinous"** and **"bulbous"** to describe me. The pressure keeps me in shape, literally speaking.

"I don't bother much with hunting for food. I just keep my rather large mouth open and close it on anything coming close. I particularly like sea urchins, sea pens, and even microscopic bacteria because I don't have any teeth to grab and chew things.

"Does my lack of muscles make me satisfied to stay wherever I happen to be? Or don't I have muscles because I don't move much? It doesn't matter as long as my lunch keeps swimming close to my mouth. That keeps me going for around 130 years.

"If you think I'm strange, have you met my friend, the jellyfish?"

Heartless and Thoughtless

"Hi, all you earth-bound creatures. Yes, I'm a jellyfish. And I'm very different from Mr. Blobby—I'm beautiful. Some wonder how I manage to be so beautiful when about 95 percent of me is water. However, the 5 percent of me that counts is made up of my almost-invisible skin, a gooey, squishy layer,

and then the place where I digest everything I eat. You may cringe, but I take in my food and let the waste out through the same hole. Did I hear someone say, "ugh"? Technically, my name is gelatinous **zooplankton**—gelata for short. Yes, I realize it sounds a bit like ice cream, but I strongly recommend you don't try to eat me for dessert.

"Unlike my blob friend, I do move around. In case you're wondering how I do it without fins or a tail, I use jet propulsion! I bring water into my body and then push it hard away from me. The pushing makes my body into a nice sleek bell shape to reduce resistance, and off I go. While the term "jet propulsion" sounds like I go fast, I'm really not terribly speedy. Nevertheless, it's quick enough for me.

"I don't have a heart, so Valentine's Day doesn't mean a whole lot to me. I don't think about it, though—or anything, to be honest —because I don't have a brain. I won't bleed to death because I don't have any blood either. A bunch of nerves make a sort of net over my body. The nerve net lets me smell things without a nose, and sense light and other happenings going on around me without eyes.

"We jellies come in all sizes and live in shallow water and the deepest part of the ocean. Some of us have only eight tentacles, and others may have hundreds. Our tentacles may be red, or blue or green, and they may be only a few feet long or stretching out behind or below us for a hundred feet or more. Sometimes we get in a fight for our lives. Then, the prudent thing to do is leave a tentacle or two behind and scurry out of there. It turns out we can go faster if we don't have all our tentacles.

"I understand you humans tend to avoid me because of my tentacles. Now, I sense you don't particularly like it if you get too close to me, and I give you a zap from them. But these long stringy things really help me. Since I don't have a brain, I don't know whether you are a friend or a foe when I touch you or you touch me. I don't have eyes, so I can't see you. The safest thing for me to do is assume maybe you'd be good for my lunch, or *you* think I would be delicious for *your* lunch. As I said, I know you are there. If my chemicals sense you, they assume you need zapping. Friend or foe? I don't wait to consider it. Each of my tentacles has tiny poisonous barbs, and they can fire in a millionth of a second. It then takes only a second for me to wrap my tentacles around what hopefully is small and put it in my mouth. Don't worry, you're too big for me to eat should I sting you.

"Just like you, we jellyfish all look different. Take my relative, the crystal jelly. It is almost transparent with long, wispy tentacles. It has over one hundred tiny organs that produce a blue-green light. It's a pretty neat feature called bioluminescence.

"At the bottom of the ocean, you'll meet a very distant relative of mine, the bloody-belly comb jelly. [*Say 'bloody-belly comb jelly' out loud three times.*] I shouldn't say the bloody-belly is a relative. Even though it is called a "jelly," and we look something alike, jellyfish and comb jellies are in different families.

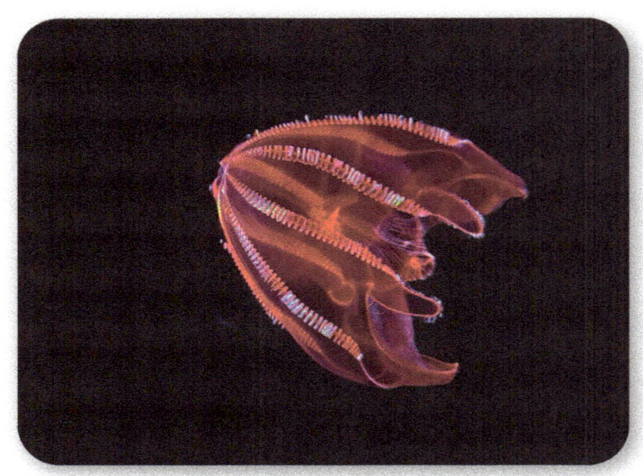

"The bloody-belly is red—no surprise there—and the color red is essential. Other parts of it may be different shades of red, but the stomach is always blood red. Most creatures down in the deep, dark bottom of the ocean can't see the color red. To them, in a place where there is no light, red looks black and is, therefore, almost invisible. Of course, the bloody-bellies ruin all the invisible effect with shimmery, rainbow-like hairs called **cilia**. They are like oars, always on the move, and they propel comb jellies through the water.

"Well, I'm getting a feeling I've rambled on long enough about myself and my cousins. Still, there's so much more to tell. Maybe later. For now, remember when I told you I don't have a brain? Okay, I admit that's a little strange, but it's not nearly as weird as my friend the sea squirt. It eats its own brain."

Hard to Swallow

"Look, Jelly, you know me eating my own brain is just a rumor."

"You don't, Squirt? Are you sure you don't eat your own brain?"

"I don't. Well, not exactly. You see, what I start out with isn't what one usually thinks of as a brain. When I'm a baby squirt, something like a tadpole, I have two things which humans call **ganglia**. They are really my 'brains.' I use one to decide where I'm going as I roam about the ocean, and the other I use to digest things and do my squirting. Digesting—that's what I do better than almost anything. Except squirting. After all, I'm not called a sea digester, am I?

"I don't roam around as a tadpole for long. As I check out my neighborhood, I soon decide where I want to stay. Perhaps an inviting rock looks appealing or a spot on the ocean floor. I settle down and attach myself, and there I am for the rest of my life. My childish, tadpolish body changes into a long tube. At the top end of the tube, I grow this rather lovely large bulge. It is then that I'm grown into a full-fledged sea squirt. I stick where I am, and I'll eat what comes by. I don't have any decisions to make. Why waste the energy on thinking? I don't need a "brain" anymore, so I digest it. I guess you could call it eating it, but I don't chew it up and swallow it. I just absorb it, and it blends into the rest of me.

"Back to the bulge I have at the top of my tube. Think of it as my head. Toward the back of it is my squirting device, where I spray enemies and dispose of my waste. At the front is my awesome mouth—toothless, but with muscles you wouldn't believe. I am a meat-eating squirt, and I'm often compared to a plant on earth called a **Venus Fly Trap**. We are a bit alike.

"Being attached securely, I can let my head float back and forth in the moving water with my mouth open. When a small animal swims close to me, my many-muscled mouth surrounds it and closes on it before it even knows what's happening. Snap! That bite is not getting away. Umm, good lunch! When I've had enough to eat, I just sort of hang out with my mouth closed.

"All of me is rather gelatinous. A bit like jello without the color. Even my blood is transparent—not red, not blue—transparent. I'm almost invisible down here in the deep ocean. If I showed up floating in a human's bedroom, which I couldn't because there's no water, they'd probably scream, 'There's a ghost in here!'

"There are other varieties of sea squirts in shallow coastal waters, all dressed up in fancy bright colors. They look a bit like a flower garden. Despite the beauty of their colors, humans consider them a big nuisance and try to find ways to get rid of them. I'm going to stay down here in the deep where I'm loved.

"I was going to introduce you to my big relative, the Giant Pyrosome. However, I see a different 'giant' is on its way over."

Arms with a Mind of Their Own

"Yes, sea squirt, I'm a giant—a Giant Pacific Octopus. And stop squirting on me. It's really unpleasant! I can't believe I'm talking to a mindless sea squirt that eats its own brain."

"I do not. Not really."

"So, did you ever have a brain?"

"Sort of."

"Do you have a brain now?"

"Maybe. Umm. Maybe not. I guess not."

"Well, I have nine brains. I've got you beat, squirt, nine times over! I can change my shape any time I feel like it. And if I get tired of swimming, I can use my arms to walk, just like legs. Can you picture it? I'm probably the most enormous octopus in the whole world, and I'm walking around on the bottom of the ocean.

"Yes, I know I said I walk on my arms. Humans seem to have a problem deciding what to call some of my parts. Some call them tentacles; some call them arms; some call them legs. What does it matter? I'm an OCTOpus, so there are eight of them.

"Having nine brains helps a lot. I have one in my head and one in each arm. Actually, they aren't all really full-fledged brains. They are **distributed intelligence**. My main brain keeps track of what's going on and doesn't interfere much with what my arms decide to do. One arm doesn't care what the other arms are doing. Sometimes my primary brain knows we all need to act together. Then it takes control, and the others follow its orders.

"My three hearts work a bit like my nine brains. I don't have any to spare. Two hearts pump blood to my gills, and a third, the largest one, pumps blood to the rest of my organs. The organ heart, by the way, stops beating when I swim. You can understand why I'd rather walk than swim.

"Humans have red blood because of the **hemoglobin** in it, but my blood is a beautiful blue. I can't use hemoglobin because of the almost-freezing, low-oxygen water I live in. Instead, I have **hemocyanin**, to carry oxygen through my system.

"Here's another thing you might find a bit strange about us octopuses. If an enemy bites off one of our arms, we can just generate another. No big deal. Actually, if we get really bored, we might eat one ourselves.

"It is possible we get bored because we have such fine big brains. We can even use tools if no one is looking, although we don't often let people see us doing it. Scientists like trying to find out what we can do, so they gave one of my sisters a childproof pill bottle. The trick is to push down and turn the cap at the same time. She opened it in five minutes. We can find our way through mazes, solve problems, and remember the solutions to those problems.

"If we want to change the color of our entire body, we can do it in three-tenths of a second! You wouldn't even see it happen. We do it because we don't carry around any protective shell. Coloring ourselves to look like a rock or coral camouflages us from our enemies.

"I'll guess humans wish they could do some of the things with their arms that I can do with mine. You may know about the 240 suckers each arm has, but did you know just *one* of the larger suckers can hold something weighing as much as thirty-five pounds? Besides being strong, they're sensitive too. They can detect the smallest chemical signals, and each one can move individually. A sucker can pinch much in the same way you pick up something with your forefinger and thumb.

"Then there's our well-known way of protection—ink. We don't squirt it out just to hide inside it; we can go into combat with it. If we squirt it in the eyes of our enemy, it will irritate so badly the attacker can't see. It also alters the ability to smell and taste. We do have to be careful with our ink, though. If we don't skedaddle fast enough, we could have been on a suicide mission. Our own ink can kill us.

"I believe I'd best be on my way. My brains tell me the viperfish swimming this way is no friend."

Making Friends Is Hard to Do

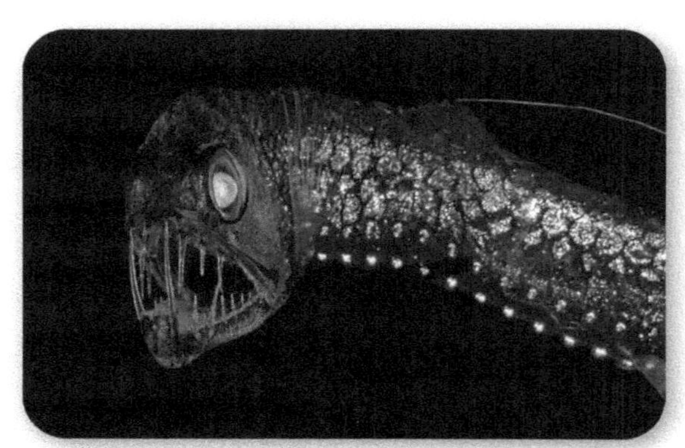

"You'd better beat it, octopus. Even with three hearts and nine brains, you can't scare anything as much as I can with only one of each. Fierce looking and sly is what we Sloane's viperfish are.

"Granted, we viperfish aren't the biggest fish in the pond. I'm less than a foot long, although some of my cousins can be as long as six feet. Some of my shorter buddies only grow to be two inches. But we have a WOW factor that can't be beat. A bunch of lights strung along our bodies flashes blue, green, and yellow by bioluminescence. Our spots of illumination come from glands called **photophores**. Some dry-earth fireflies can generate light the same way.

"It's dark where I hang out in the lower levels of the twilight zone, and my spots of colored lights seem to make other fish curious. They come my way to check out the show. Bad decision—for them. Even if they would make a huge mouthful, I can unhinge my jaw and drop it open to snatch a good-sized lunch. I can also lure passers-by with an antenna I have on the top of my head. It has its own light at the tip, and I can swing it back and forth in front of my mouth to tempt the reluctant visitors.

"My mouth is filled with very sharp teeth you don't want to mess with. Trust me. And those teeth are so long I can't even close my mouth all the way. Some of my meals are bigger than I am. When my unhinged mouth snaps closed, trapping the prey I've enticed, it is a pretty strong wallop to my spine. Luckily, I have a shock absorber in my first vertebrae.

"Depending on the size of my meal, I can go for days before I have to wiggle my brilliant body and wait for another lanternfish or bristlemouth to come by. I don't move much at all in search of food. It delivers itself to me.

"As a matter of fact, I think I'm getting hungry. While I'm keeping my eyes open for a meal, here comes someone else you might find interesting. This anglerfish is *almost* as terrifying as I am. Although I think its other name is more fitting. It's goosefish!"

I'm *Alluring*

"Get out of my way, viperfish. Maybe I should make you my lunch. I could, you know. I see you very well with my searchlight. My searchlight is kindly provided me by bioluminescent bacteria. It's a nice arrangement. Those tiny friends just hang out on the end of my lure, and I don't show their light unless there is a reason to. I keep it covered with a flap of skin so I can be more stealthy.

"The thing is, the same searchlight helping me see in the dark can lure the

fish I love to eat straight to my mouth. Now, check out my mouth. It's BIG! I can actually eat something twice my size. My bones are flexible, and I can expand my stomach. So if something looks good to me, I can probably swallow it. With my long sharp teeth, I don't let anything get away once I chomp down on it. Some of us anglerfish grow to be three feet long.

"I have another advantage over most of the creatures down here at the bottom of the ocean. I can walk! My **pelvic** and **pectoral** fins act just like the legs of a dog on earth.

Bristlemouth Fish

How is a viperfish so confident it can stay parked and soon one of its favorite foods, the bristlemouth fish, will come along to satisfy its appetite? It's a pretty good guess because bristlemouths are the most abundant fish in the ocean. Scientists estimate there are more bristlemouths swimming about in the sea than there are rats, chickens, and humans combined running around on earth. At latest count—well, really, no one has counted them—there are (drum roll, please) trillions or maybe even quadrillions of them!

"I have lots of cousins. There are more than 200 species of anglerfish. Here is my close relative, the 'grumpy goosefish.'"

Grumpy? Goosy? Fishy? Which?

"'Grumpy' goosefish? Grumpy is not really my name. Nevertheless, it's what people call this side of our family. I've been told I look like I need a shave. However, my 'whiskers,' along with the spots and frilly belly area, are a good camouflage.

"We goosefish don't go searching for our prey. We simply settle down and wait until our lure attracts a meal. We have two fin rays between our eyes and dangle one or both of them like lighted fishing poles right in front of our mouth. Our awesome big, wide jaws have lots and lots of very long, very sharp teeth. When a tasty bite swims up to examine our tempting fin rays, we goosefish will have it in a nanosecond. We have one of the fastest attacks of any known fish.

"One creature down here in the depths, though, I don't want to start a fight with. I see two huge eyes looking this way now, and I'm sure there's a colossal squid attached to them. Bye!"

Not Bragging, but I'm Colossal!

"Yes, I am a colossal squid. 'Grumpy' might scare some, but not me. Never me.

"I have to laugh. The goosefish 'saw my eyes.' How could he miss them? I have the most humongous eyes in the world. I've heard some of your scientists think I have the biggest eyes in the history of the animal kingdom. Each of my eyeballs is almost as

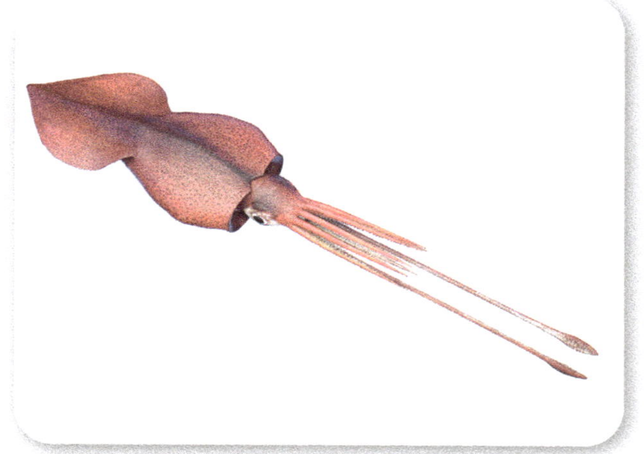

big as one of your soccer balls! Critters can see them down here in the dark because I have a light behind each eye. The lights are produced by photophores and are on all the time.

"If you're wondering why I'm not a 'giant' squid, it's because we 'colossal' squids are more than giant. Okay, a giant squid might say it's longer, and I have to admit some of them are, but we are a lot heavier and bigger around. Don't demote me to the size of a mere giant!

"I don't eat much, and I tear up whatever I eat into little bite-size pieces. I have to take small bites of my food, or it could damage my brain. Why could the size of my food damage my brain? It may seem a bit absurd considering my overall enormousness, but my brain is not very big, and it's shaped like a doughnut with a hole in the center. Stop laughing! My esophagus, or throat, runs through that fairly small hole. So, if I eat something too big, it rubs against my brain and could injure it. Please don't offer me any of your ice cream. I might get brain freeze!

"A mound of thirty small paper clips is about the amount of food I eat in a day. If you'd put it on a scale, it would weigh about the same as a slice of your bread—somewhere around an ounce and a half.

"I hope you're not one of those earth-walkers who identify me with an octopus. Octopuses have eight tentacles. I have eight arms, and two tentacles—a big difference. At least, I think it is.

"Both my tentacles are longer than my arms, and my arms are all different lengths. The shortest one may not reach three feet, while the longest could be almost four feet (0.85 to 1.15 meters). All the suckers on my arms have saw-like edges. I have a double row of hooks in the middle of each arm, with suckers above and below them. Each hook

has one large main claw and two smaller ones. When I use my arms to hold my selection from the day's menu, it doesn't get away.

Squid Fiber

You just read about the sharp teeth in the suction cups of squid tentacles. They are made of a substance able to take a lot of wear and tear and last for a long time. They can even heal themselves. Proteins in those teeth are responsible for their unique qualities, but there are so few of them it isn't worth the cost and effort to harvest. The thing is, those proteins are a lot like silk made by spiders, but having been made in water, they don't shrink in water the way spider silk has a tendency to do.

Researchers went to the drawing board and found a way to reproduce the proteins and make a mash from them. It is then dried into a powder and spun with water into strands of fiber. The resulting thread is called Squitex. By combining it with other products, it becomes biodegradable.

"I catch my lunch with my tentacles. They don't just have suckers on them—by each sucker is a very sharp hook. These tentacle hooks are very different from those I have on my arms. These can rotate 360 degrees. You can imagine the difference it makes grabbing and holding on to my prey with those rotating hooks. My catch can wriggle all it wants, and my hooks just swivel around with it. They are smaller than the hooks on my arms, and they aren't three-pointed. So once I snag some sea creature, I have no problem holding on to it. My tentacles bring it up to my mouth. Then, I just rip it apart with my beak into those tiny bites I need to be able to swallow.

I digest my food very slowly. A good-sized fish, say about fifty pounds, can last me for more than half a year.

"Your scientists don't know a lot about me yet. I manage to be rather elusive. Maybe you and I could become friends, and I might let you learn more of my secrets. Be prepared to dodge my arms and tentacles, though. I admit I'm not very courteous. And you can bet I don't fall apart at the least little clash with one of my water-wandering enemies like this pyrosome might."

My, What a Big Mouth You Have!

"Okay, okay, Squidy. So what if I'm a bit on the delicate side? Pyrosome means fire (pyro) and body (soma), so fire body. At least it sounds kind of fearsome. We giant pyrosomes emit a bluish-greenish bioluminescent light. You might be able to see us if you are even 100 feet away. If you do see us, please try to avoid us.

"It's pretty amazing, for even though pyrosomes look like one creature, we are actually hundreds, sometimes thousands, of individual buds known as **zooids**. Each zooid is a clone of another. Although a zooid looks something like the sea squirt, it can be smaller than a jellybean. All those zooids, or clones, are separate, complete animals. Joined together, they form a **colony**. These colonies form me, the pyrosome, and I can grow up to sixty feet long. They reproduce by making exact copies of themselves, called cloning. If they get hurt, they just replace the damaged zooids by growing new ones. Unless all the clones are killed at the same time, I could

probably live forever.

"I, the full pyrosome, and all my zooids, are gelatinous. Everybody is held together with a **viscous tunic**. We are all part of the tunicate family because of our tunics. Calling us tunicates makes sense when you know about the tunics, doesn't it? Pyrosomes have a point on one end and a giant mouth on the other. Our mouth can be six feet across and big enough to gobble up a human. We look a bit like an enormous windsock—a huge string of jelly that could close its lips around you in one gulp. We probably wouldn't, though.

"We don't fasten ourselves onto anything to stay in one place. All our zooids squirt jets of water in unison, pushing us around while we search for food.

"If you could touch me, I would feel like a long fluffy scarf, delicate and fragile. Because we are bioluminescent, we can be quite beautiful. When something touches me, my zooids shine blue, green, red, or white lights through the darkness of the ocean. All of me glows as the light wave passes from one zooid to another, indicating possible danger. When the light show begins, the squirting pushing me through the water stops, and we all sink down, out of harm's way.

"Pyrosomes often hang out in groups. When other pyrosome colonies in a group see the bioluminescence of another, they stop swimming and also begin to light up. They, too, drop downward in the black ocean."

[*What a sight it must be to see all those brightly glowing animals descending through their watery home. Maybe it's their version of a Fourth of July fireworks display, where you'd go "Oooh" and "Ahhh."*]

"Pardon my smirk. Do you understand now why sea squirts are proud to have pyrosomes in their family? It's too bad the Giant Pacific Octopus had to intrude or we'd have met sooner.

"On the other hand, we have a friend down here you might think is a close member of my family. For all practical purposes,

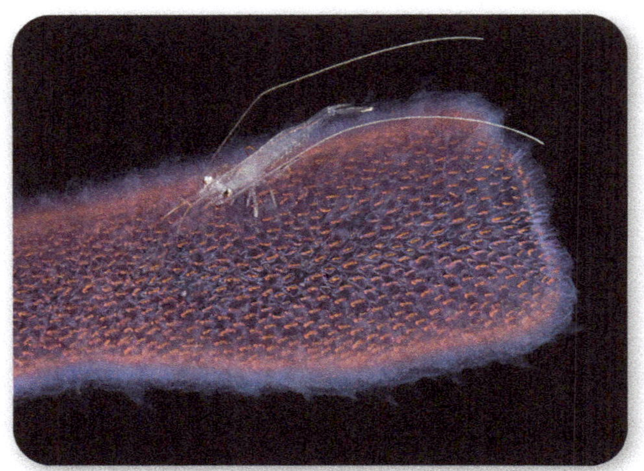

though, we are not related at all. I'm talking about the siphonophore. I believe I see one on its way over to babble with you now."

Delicate Dancers

"Hi, pyro. We siphonophores do have a lot in common with you pyrosomes. However, if one looks at the diagram of creatures, you are a **Chordata**, and I am a

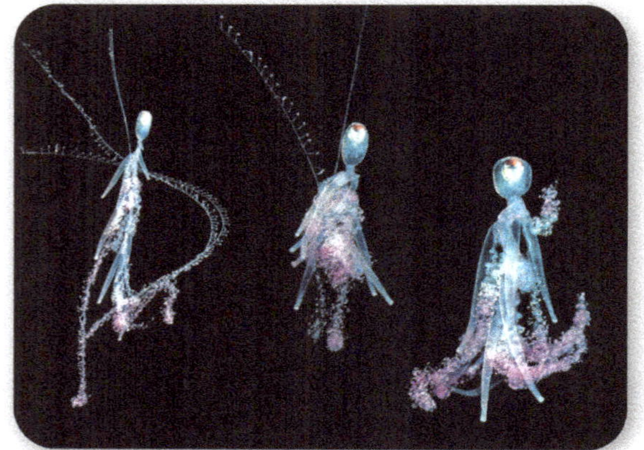

Cnidaria. It seems a shame to me you are grouped with humans only because you have a nerve cord as a tiny tadpole. Even that is just for just a blink in time. If you had any backbone, you would deny you were entitled to the designation. I'm proud to say we siphonophores are more closely related to corals and jellyfish than pyrosomes or humans.

"Like you, pyrosomes, I'm squishy and a bit jelly-like. I also have more parts than probably anyone cares to count. We are called 'colonial' because we have a colony of small zooids—again, like the pyrosome. Each zooid is an individual, but it is attached to the others. You may be wondering how parts can be individual and attached to each other at the same time. It's complicated.

"Every one of my little zooids, each looking a bit like a small flower, has its own job to do. It can't do anything else. One type moves me, the whole siphonophore, through the water. You humans call it swimming. However, the swimmer zooids can't catch our food. The ones catching prey can't eat it. Those responsible for eating can't swim. Every different kind of zooid I have relies on all the others to live.

"Not only that, each of my zooids had better be in the right place. They can't just randomly grow here or there. Think of us as being a little, a *very* little, like the parts of you humans. You have a brain, lungs, heart, blood cells, and muscles. Each has a unique work assignment, and they all have specific locations. They can't decide to move to another place in your body. Your ear wouldn't function well as a tongue. Do you see how much we're alike? Well, I admit saying we're 'alike' may be stretching the point.

"Speaking of stretching, I can keep growing and growing and growing. Some of us have grown to be 130 feet (40 meters) long. Did you ever see a blue whale? It's the biggest animal in the world, and I am even longer! I have to admit the blue whale is a bit bigger around than I am. If you ever swept the leaves off your sidewalk, you know what a broomstick looks like. That's me. I'm about as big around as a broomstick.

"I told you before, I'm a relative of jellyfish. One of the ways I'm like them is my ability to shine with colored light—you know, bioluminescence. I happen to be able to shine with a blue light. Some of us can glow green, and occasionally some might glimmer orange or red. Others aren't bioluminescent at all.

"Another characteristic I share with jellyfish is my ability to sting. My many tentacles trap prey and stab them with poison. It immediately takes them out of the action, and my meal is ready to eat.

"I mustn't forget about my cousin. I wonder if you saw it when you first came down by the hydrothermal vent—you know, the chimney-like thing spouting extremely hot water. All kinds of animals like to live there, like giant tube worms, clams, shrimp, and my cousin, the dandelion siphonophore."

Hands Off, I'm Fragile

"I heard scientists named me for a plant you have on the dry earth, but

we dandelion siphonophores are definitely not plants. I'm an animal all the way. Along with looking a lot different than I do, my siphonophore cousins swim around. I don't. I fasten myself tight and stay in one place all my life. Although it may sound rather boring to you ordinary siphonophores, you shouldn't criticize something you've never tried.

"Some lab people attempted to take one of us up to earth in a container they specially designed to care for a dandelion siphonophore. It didn't work. The one they wanted to study fell totally apart. It completely disintegrated when it got up into your air, like cotton candy in your mouth. We siphonophores are very delicate creatures, after all.

"Wait! What is that yammering? It sounds like a whispered shout."

This Bears Investigating

"It's me, Dandy. Don't let our friends miss out on meeting me just because I'm so much smaller than almost everyone else.

"Nice to see you, friends of us extremophiles. Well, really, I'm not seeing you. You're seeing me, and probably through a microscope. I'm kind of small—about the size of the period at the end of this sentence. That's why it took until late in the 1700s, after microscopes were invented, for my German friend, August Goeze, to go nuts about me.

"What was a German pastor looking for through his microscope in 1773? I've no idea. My guess is he was curious about what he might see through the new-fangled invention. Then, when he found me, he fell in love. Wouldn't you? He called me his 'little water bear.'

"There was an Italian biologist later on who also found me with his microscope and called me *Tardigrada*. It means 'slow stepper' or 'slow walker.' I don't think he had a proper appreciation for my cuteness. Even though the name tardigrade stuck, I still prefer little water bear.

"I admit, I'm sort of round and plump and have eight stubby legs, but I'm tougher than you might expect.

"Drop me on an iceberg in the Antarctic, and I won't need a coat. I don't even shiver in −300° F (−185° C).

"Toss me into the vacuum of outer space without a spacesuit. I'll keep on paddling.
'I can stand radiation over 1,000 times what you humans can tolerate.

"You can dump me without a submersible vehicle to the bottom of the deep, deep, deepest place on the entire earth, where pressure turns most earthly things to slush—I'll keep poking my snout out and in, searching for food.

"While I'm down there at the bottom of the ocean, I might nestle up next to a vent where the water temperature can be a sizzling 300° F. I'll sigh, relax, and feel like I'm in a fancy spa.

"Plop me in the middle of a barren desert, and I won't care. I can go for thirty years without food or water. No matter how extreme the living conditions, I can survive it all! I guess I deserve being called an extremophile.

"Do you know how I can handle all those extremes? It's a pretty neat trick. If the temperature, or pressure, or radiation, or whatever is more than I can endure, I just roll up into a tiny ball called a 'tun.' While I'm rolling up, I squeeze out as much of the water in me as I can. I just relax and let time go by until my environment is pleasant again, relatively speaking. Then I unroll and paddle away.

I'm proud to say we tardigrades have been awarded the title 'The Most Extreme Survivor.' We were up against tough competition, but we beat out Antarctic penguins, the super-dry-desert camels, and even that disgusting cockroach. All, while being cute.

"You can watch me swim if you go to the internet video you'll find listed at the back of this book. You'll laugh to see my snout go out and in to suck up food. If you fall completely in love with me, there are even stuffed plush water bears!"

<<>>

It's time to leave these cute and cuddly (well, maybe not so cuddly) creatures of the deep dark ocean. We need to find out about some of their beneficial qualities. Some of these may surprise you.

"Wait! No, don't go! I didn't know you cared about what medical marvels we water bears can accomplish, despite our small size. Let me tell you."

Extremely Handy to Have Around

"I'm more than a cute little extremophile. I may be able to help you in ways humans can't. Remember the neat little trick I told you about? How I can roll up into a tun when the environment is too cold, or too hot, or too dry, or there is too much radiation?

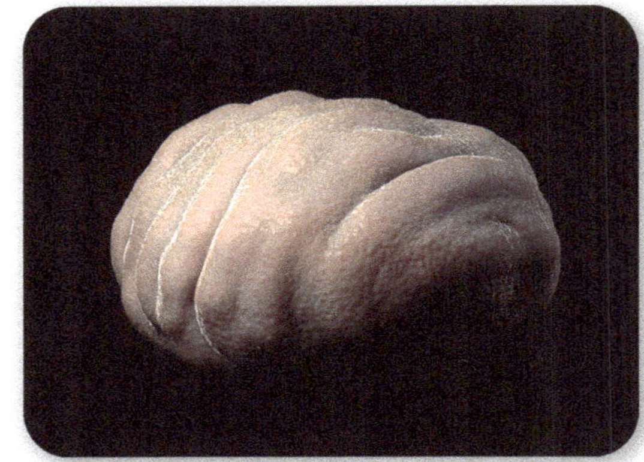

"What if one of you, you human creatures, needed a lot of radiation to treat a disease? Sometimes it's the best or only way to treat cancer. I've heard you don't handle radiation as well as I do. Researchers took a gene of mine, put it in some human kidney cells, and discovered the radiation didn't do nearly as much damage. They're trying to find a way to give my genes to you so you can survive, too.

"We could even help with exploration of space. Earth's atmosphere protects humans from the radiation of the sun. That protection is lost out in space. If they can figure out how we can endure so much radiation without damaging effects, they might be better able to help astronauts survive it."

"Excuse me, Water Bear. May I ask a question?"

"Sure, Dandy. What is it?"

"Why would humans want to go out into space? There's no water, no oxygen, and radiation that can kill them."

"I can see why you wouldn't understand, Dandy, since you're tied down to one place, but it's exciting to see and feel different places. You can learn a lot traveling about. Even discovering how to survive is interesting—and challenging. If humans didn't like adventure, they wouldn't come down to learn about us. That would be sad for both them and us.

"In addition to enduring a lot of radiation, there are other things tardigrades can help with. Often doctors need to preserve biological material like tissues for transplants and blood for transfusions. Storing those may be more successful if they can figure out what makes us able to survive a long time in harsh circumstances.

"There are a lot of diseases scientists are looking into with the idea we cute little water bears may be able to help. We're so unusual they have to know physics, chemistry, and biology to understand how we do what we do."

It Doesn't Take a Brain

"Hey there, Water Bear. Don't make people think you're the only one down here in the deep able to help them."

"Hi, Squirty. I didn't see you over there. Are you telling me you can help humans, too?"

"You better believe it. We sea squirts and pyrosomes have an ingredient in us that may cure several types of solid tumors. It can also be used to fight leukemia. Sea squirts can help a lot, even if we do eat our own brains."

I See a Sea Sponge

"Water Bear! Water Bear! Where have you been? I wanted to get in this conversation, but just like Squirty, I can't move from this spot."

"Coming. I tend to forget most of us ocean creatures with medically useful chemicals are generally **sessile**. You fasten yourselves tight and don't move around. You stay-at-homers seem to have the most chemicals to fight off predators. Who are you? I don't think we've met."

"My real name is Dysidea sp., but why don't you just call me Dizzy? As you can see, I'm a sponge. I'm sort of the representative of a lot of our sponge community.

"As you said, it's hard to fight for your life when you're just a porous, rather dull-colored blobby clump stuck in one spot. Chemicals are our go-to protection.

"Did you see the human the other day who was wandering around in the water? She was actually looking for us sea sponges. And it wasn't just for wiping her sink or taking a bath, Water Bear."

"No? What else would humans do with a sponge?"

"It's our *chemicals*, you tiny **desiccated** multi-extremical creature!"

"Hey, I'm not desiccated now. I'm round and plump. At least I can go wherever I want."

"Maybe so, but the human wasn't looking for you. She wanted me! She found a way to help other humans by using my chemicals to fight all sorts of their diseases like cancer, chickenpox, and shingles. One of us sponge-kind can even put a brake on cancer cells' growth while letting normal cells continue to grow."

"What happens when humans have used up all you sponges to get those super chemicals? I guess you'll be long gone."

"Humans are smarter than you think, Water Bear. Their scientists are making copies of our chemicals so they can grow them in a laboratory. They're even thinking of farming us."

"Well, for your sake, Dizzy, I hope it works."

"I understand we sponges are not alone in having chemicals helpful to humans. I hear dry-earthers do something called 'breathing', and some can't do it very well. It's a disease called asthma."

"They breathe? They take in oxygen like we do?"

"No, not like we do, they don't have gills, and they don't live in water. Remember it's dry up there."

"Amazing. I wonder how they do that. But back to what you were saying about asthma and sponges."

"It's not only us sponges, Water Bear. Even coral and some others of us living in this water world produce a substance to help treat asthma."

Sponges Leave a Trail

Are sponges sessile, or can they move about? The answer, it seems, is 'yes' and 'yes'. Researchers were looking at some photographs of the ocean floor, and they saw paths ending at a bunch of sponges. They were as certain as they could be sponges don't move around. Still, here were their trails. It seems they must be able to move, but the pace is not very fast—just a few centimeters a year. Who do you suppose figured that out and how? Hopefully not by continuously watching one.

What Do Sponges Do in Their Spare Time?

They pump water. Not just a little water. A lot of water. Sponges can pump an amount of water 10,000 times their own size by volume in one day. Do you or your friend have a swimming pool in the backyard? A sponge about the size of a football helmet could pump enough water to fill it in one day! And they can snag and hold on to 90 percent of all bacteria in the water filtering through them.

Call Me Pete

"You're forgetting about malaria."

"Who said that?"

"It's me. Over here, Water Bear. Dizzy isn't the only sponge in the ocean, you know."

"I'm sorry for ignoring you. What's your name?"

"Technically, I'm Petroside Ng5 Sp5. Let's shorten it to Pete."

"Nice to meet you, Pete. You wanted to say something about malaria?"

"Well, up on dry earth there are flying creatures called mosquitoes. They carry a sickness known as malaria, and over 200 million people get it every year. More than 400,000 of them will die. We sponges may hold the key to cure it. There are a lot of other parasitic diseases we may also be able to cure.

"Oops. Here comes something I don't have a cure for. Hey, you there. Cone snail. You can stop right there."

Baddest of the Bad

"Oh, don't worry, Pete. I know none of you are going to try to eat me."

"Well, why don't you just stay a good little distance away? You can shoot out your long, flexible snout faster than I can see it. You know what that means."

"Yes. It means you'd be dead. I promise I won't zap you. I just want to let you know what the poisons I carry can do. Other than make you dead, of course."

"Okay, but still, stay your distance. There are almost no creatures with venom as toxic as yours, Coney."

"Did you know my little six-inch body carries about 100 different poisons? Humans, like the one looking for you sponges, think they can use them. They seem to make great painkillers. If a human should step on me, they might not even feel it. Maybe just a little numbness or tingling. Give the poison a little while to spread through their body, and there is almost no way to stop it or get it out."

"So, Coney, why is this a good thing for humans?"

"Their scientists found some of my chemicals are 1,000 times stronger than morphine for killing pain, and they aren't addictive. If someone is in a lot of pain, they'd be grateful to get a shot of my poison.

"Having a great painkiller is not the only reason I fascinate humans. The more they study my chemicals, the more illnesses, they realize, will be helped by them. One of my chemicals is a fast-acting form of insulin. That is the drug they use when someone has diabetes. Other conditions they think will benefit are epilepsy, asthma, Alzheimer's, Parkinson's, and multiple sclerosis.

"What's bad for both the humans and us is, we cone snails are disappearing. About ten percent of us are on the endangered, vulnerable, or near threatened list."

Not a Bread Spread

"Hey, is there room for a jelly in this discussion?"

"Sure. Just keep your tentacles to yourself."

"Of course, Water Bear, although I see Coney's over there. I'm a pushover compared to it."

"What brings you here?"

"I heard you talking about all the benefits we lovely denizens of the deep have. I didn't know if you'd heard about what some of those dry-earth people are learning they can do with my specialty—bioluminescence."

"What? Bioluminescence is light. What does you glowing in the dark do for humans?"

"You'll be surprised. We all know different elements in many of us can help humans. Some of you have been talking about treating cancer. Well, we bioluminescent jellyfish have proteins that make us glow. When scientists take the green fluorescent protein— they call it GFP for short—and put it in human cancer cells, it lights up. They can see where the cancer is. I heard GFP even helps doctors better understand Alzheimer's, HIV, and Ebola.

"Several varieties of us jellies help people heal. There is a story about hydra jellies. They live in fresh water, not here in the ocean. Some humans say they can chop up a hydra in a blender, and its pieces will creep and crawl their way back together again and be good as new!"

"Yuck! Really?"

"So I hear. But that's not all. We jellyfish are often described as 'gelatinous' because we're made up mostly of collagen. Research is moving right along to use our collagen to help with osteoarthritis and other diseases. Another advantage is if humans decide to use us for our medical benefits, they won't easily be able to endanger us. The ocean warming helps us reproduce, so there are more and more of us to supply their needs.

"Where are you going, Water Bear? I didn't accidentally zap you, did I?"

"I have to get a move on. I can't just sit around all day like all these sessile creatures. It's been a fun discussion, though.

"Let me introduce a couple of humans who find our ocean intriguing: Laura Bagge and Eric Stackpole."

Can I Be an Oceanographer?

You may be thinking oceanography seems to be important and necessary, as well as being a fun way to spend your life, however, you've never even seen the ocean. Or you may live near the ocean, and the thought of going down deep in it terrifies you. Or you may not be the best student in your class, and you don't know how you'd get all the education you need. Or you are a girl, and you think there are not many women oceanographers. Those are logical feelings for you to have. Let's see if anyone else faced those same problems.

In Their Own Words
Laura Bagge

BS Marine Biology, summa cum laude, MS Marine Biology, PhD Biology General; Postdoctoral Researcher Air Force Research Laboratory and UF REEF; NRC Postdoctoral Fellow, Air Force Research Laboratory

Q. Where did you grow up? Was it near a lake or the ocean?

I grew up in Knoxville, Tennessee, which is about an eight-hour drive away from the ocean! My mom and I would make the trip from Knoxville to Emerald Isle, North Carolina, every year for a one-week beach vacation!

Q. Did growing up near the ocean play any part in your career decision?

Growing up and going to the beach every year played a big role in my decision to study marine biology! I loved being at the beach more than anything else. When I was only 13, I begged my mom to get certified to scuba dive with me. We got certified to scuba dive in a rock quarry in the middle of Tennessee, where it was cold, dark, and the visibility was so bad you couldn't see a few inches past your face. But it was all worth it when we finally went scuba diving for the first time on a shipwreck off the coast of North Carolina and saw so many cool animals!

Q. What interested you as a kid?

While I did get certified to scuba dive when I was only 13 years old, I wasn't sure I was going to be a scientist back then. I thought I was going to be an actor. I took tons of acting classes and tried out for every school and community play. Learning how to speak to an audience has come in handy now that I give lots of public presentations about science.

Q. How did you get started in this field?

I guess you could say I got started in the field of marine biology and oceanography when I got certified to scuba dive at age 13, but I certainly didn't understand then what a marine biology career would be like. I'd say I really got started in the field during my first year of college at the University of North Carolina Wilmington. I took a lot of great classes with professors who involved the students in their research. I got to have hands-on experience in conducting science experiments.

Q. What was your first trip in Alvin like?

My first trip in Alvin was absolutely life-changing and a dream come true. I had been studying a really weird ocean animal called Phronima for a few years. It's a totally transparent crustacean. I had never seen one swimming around in the open ocean before though. Previously, I had been able to catch them in a large net we would drag behind a boat and bring to the surface. Being in Alvin, I was able to observe this animal through the porthole window! It was fantastic.

If you want to know more about this experience, you can watch me talk about my dive in Alvin at:

https://www.youtube.com/watch?v=dxECR6SjVbU
Or read more about the story here:
https://stories.duke.edu/exploring-earths-inner-space-submarine.

Q. Where are you working now?

I'm working at the Air Force Research Laboratory, which is located on the Gulf Coast of Florida.

Q. What is your favorite part of what you are doing now?

My job now involves conducting lots of basic research about how animals see and avoid being seen. You never know what new discoveries can be made simply from observing a weird animal, and the ocean is certainly the place filled with the weirdest animals, in my opinion!

Q. What would you say to kids to interest them in choosing oceanography as a career?

I would say choosing oceanography as a career can be hard work, but it's totally worth it! My mom and I bought matching T-shirts from my undergraduate university, University of North Carolina Wilmington, which had the following quote on it: "One cannot discover new oceans without the courage to lose sight of shore!" I've always loved that quote. I don't know who the original author is. I think this quote sums up what it's like to be in oceanography or marine biology as a career!

The biggest inspiration in my life is my mom, who sadly passed away before I got my PhD. To honor her legacy, I wrote down my memories of going to the beach with her and entered it into a contest to win a free week at the beach at Emerald Isle, North Carolina! I won! Thanks again, Mom!

Eric Stackpole

BS Mechanical Engineering and MS Mechanical Engineering; Co-Founder SoFar Ocean Technologies; Co-Founder OpenROV; Pilot and Mechanical Engineer for the SCINI (Submersible Capable of under Ice Navigation and Imaging) Project; NASA Small Spacecraft Design; Starring in National Geographic Ocean Exploration Series produced by James Cameron

When asked if he would share his background for this book, Eric Stackpole said his main reason for agreeing to do it was to give hope to some of the kids who might be below-average students. Still in his mid-30s, he has a remarkably successful career, although it came at a price. He was willing to pay that price—to work hard for the education he needed.

<<>>

Q: Tell me a little about yourself. You are a highly successful man. What is the driving force in your life?

Of all the things I feel passionate about and want to work toward is the single notion that I want people to find their superpowers. Even if they don't fit into the box in school, there may be other things they can do well. I think it's such an important and critical part of someone's life. Even more than the specific education they are getting is forming a feeling of self-identity. "Who am I? Who can I become? What are my interests?"

Q: As a boy, you had difficulties learning. What were your problems?

I'll tell you because I'm really not ashamed of it. I think it's important. I was held back in 2nd grade. I was in special ed throughout a lot of elementary school. I had documented learning disabilities. I got extra time on tests.

I remember my third-grade teacher brought an electrical plate, batteries and light bulbs. She let us try to configure them. Maybe it was just by chance I figured out this thing that everyone was trying to build, but I got it to work! For the first time ever, I really had the feeling, "Hey, maybe this is something I'm all right at."

Q: It sounds like that gave you the confidence you needed to know you were able to learn.

I realize not all people are the same. I inherently have a lot of curiosity. I know a lot of other kids do, too. Some people really do want structure. They want to be told, "This is a new thing. This is how it works." They enjoy the process of learning by instruction. But there's no single way you can teach all students. Everyone has a

different learning style. I feel it's the responsibility of teachers, parents, and the people around them to help find how they're going to learn best. I think kids should be aware people learn in different ways; they can find ways they will do much better, acknowledge those, and pursue them.

If you're in an environment where you don't like to learn, not only are you not learning as well, you're feeling the discouragement from everyone else doing so well. "How can they all be doing so well when I'm doing so poorly?" You feel like, "Wow, I must really be stupid."

Q: You have a need to learn with 'hands-on.' How were you able to get both a bachelor's and a master's degree? That's a lot of 'book learning.'

I struggled through college. It was a slog the entire time. The only thing that kept me going was my genuine love of engineering. I found a genuine passion.

It's what I'm thinking about when I'm in the shower, or when I'm stuck in traffic, or on a walk—I'm thinking about how can you build something.

Q: Did anything special influence your choice of colleges after high school?

One of the main reasons I chose San Jose State was because they had a project to actually build a satellite. However, the satellite project was run by the aerospace department, and I was a mechanical engineer. They said, "You have to be an aerospace engineer." I thought, *The heck with this, I'll just start my own club and build a satellite of our own.* Starting the satellite club got the attention of the people at NASA and got me the job at NASA.

At NASA, people said, "Most of us have graduate degrees. You really ought to have a graduate degree. Why don't we help you get into a grad lab?" Also, I became interested when I saw what they were doing with ROVs.

Q: Now you're working with National Geographic and James Cameron. How exciting.

The National Geographic series is about ocean exploration. It has the working title Mission OceanX or Ocean Xplorers, and the ship is called the Ocean Xplorer.

As a mechanical engineer, I have a lot of experience creating underwater exploration gadgets. I'm one of the four main characters in this series—the gadget guy. There are two scientists on board who get into the big questions we're trying to answer. The fourth has a background in the military and handles the logistics of the expedition.

Q: Do you work on a stage set or are you on a ship?

We're on a ship, and the ship was built for the show. It is the most advanced research vessel and media platform that has ever existed on the planet! The Ocean Xplorer 1 is over 280 feet long. Its two manned submersibles can go more than 3,000 feet (1,000 meters) deep. They have a big transparent acrylic sphere—when you're in it, you can look at all directions around you.

It's difficult to describe the emotions of going down there. It's not just a change in scenery, it's a change in mood. Picture being at the surface in this sub. They pick you off the deck of the ship with a crane, and they put you in the water, with divers in inflatable boats, and they're checking off and detaching hooks and ropes, and then you're set free from the ship, and you're bouncing around, and all the waves hitting the vents unit, and all of a sudden the sub starts to dive.

Before you know it you're looking up, and there's ocean above you, and these waves start crashing around, turbid, and as you get deeper and deeper, the hanger deck gets farther away from you. And it starts getting quieter. And more gentle. And the movement of the sea becomes slower. As you go deeper and deeper, it seems like time itself is slowing down.

My first dive was shallower, only 200 meters. When we got to the bottom, you could still see a little bit of glow, a kind of blue coming from above, but it was mostly dark. Then the sub sat down, and it just felt quiet, more gentle. It felt like time goes more slowly. What we watched happening in front of us could be part of the process that had been happening for thousands of years, and we just never really bothered to know it. The majority of our own planet—we just have no idea what's down there.

Seeing it firsthand is an emotional experience. It's not just about gathering the data; it's about realizing we've been taking for granted what is there all the time.

<<>>

Does this sound like an exciting life? Something you would like to experience? Then check at the back of this book for the list of studies you might want to take in college, and begin to set your goals now. Read all you can about the variety of specializations in oceanography. See if there are any programs open to students of your age to give you a taste of what happens at the bottom of the ocean. Write a letter to an oceanographer and ask questions. Who knows, you might find a mentor out there.

Glossary

Bioluminescence

'Bio' means having to do with a living creature, and 'luminescence' is the production or emission of light. Therefore, bioluminescence is the production of light by a living creature.

Bulbous

Fat, round, bulging—a glance at the blobfish out of the water, and you get the picture.

Certification

A certification gives official approval that someone or something can safely or properly do what it claims.

Chemosynthesis

Chemosynthesis is the combination of organic elements by bacteria or other similar life forms. They use energy from reactions involving inorganic chemicals, typically in the absence of sunlight.

Chordata

In the Chordata family are vertebrate animals, including sea squirts. They have a stem or rod made of a substance similar to cartilage, called a notochord, at some point in their development, which qualifies them as a vertebrate for their lifetime.

Cilia (plural of cilium)

Cilia are tiny threads projecting from a cell or organism. They move rhythmically to move the organism through a fluid.

Cnidaria

The family known as Cnidaria has more than 9,000 species. Most are aquatic invertebrate animals. They do not have a backbone. They have a simple net-like nervous system. This group of animals includes sea anemones, corals, and jellyfish.

Colony

A colony can be a group of humans, animals, or organisms living together and depending on each other.

Desiccated

If something is desiccated, it is all dried out, like tardigrades become when they are in an unfriendly environment and roll up into a tun.

Distributed Intelligence

The intelligence provided separately from the central brain allows the octopus' arms to problem-solve independently.

Extremophiles

Extremophiles can exist in conditions impossible for humans, such as extremely high temperatures and extremely high pressure. Those are extreme only from a human point of view.

Ganglia

This is the plural form of ganglion. Ganglia are a network of cells that form a nerve center in an invertebrate.

Gelatinous

When something is gelatinous, it resembles gelatin or jelly. It may also be gummy, sticky, or slimy.

Hemocyanin

Hemocyanin is a protein in the blood of arthropods and mollusks. It contains copper, and transports oxygen in the blood plasma.

Hemoglobin

Hemoglobin is a protein in blood carrying oxygen throughout the body.

Hydrothermal Vent

This one you may have figured out yourself. Hydro is water. You drink water for hydration, especially in the summer. Thermal relates to temperature, like in thermometer. A vent is a hole that releases matter.

Manipulator Arm

A manipulator arm on a submersible robot has a wide range of motions. It can raise and rotate its shoulder, bend its elbow, and the wrist can move up, down, rotate and grip. There is a 'master control' on the ship to move the arm under the ocean.

Microbes

These creatures were originally given the name microbes because they were thought to be visible only through a microscope. Generally a microbe or microorganism can refer to bacteria, fungi, viruses and protozoa.

Midnight Zone

This is also known as the 'bathypelagic zone'. It reaches from a point (roughly) 3,300 feet (1,000 meters) beneath the surface of the ocean to about 13,100 feet (4,000 meters). It is often referred to as the midnight zone because of its constant darkness.

Panoramic

If a photograph or a view is said to be panoramic, it means it has a wide, sweeping view.

Pelvic

The pelvis (pelvic area) is the lower or back part of the trunk, depending on the animal. It is just above or in front of the legs.

Pectoral Fin

Pectoral fins are located underneath a fish. They help the fish keep its balance, stay level, and keep it from rolling from side to side.

Photophores

Photophores are organs that light up. The light, also called bioluminescence, can attract prey, be used as a searchlight, and hide the silhouette of the creature from a predator.

Photosynthesis

Photosynthesis is the process plants use to take in carbon dioxide (CO_2) and water (H_2O), capturing energy from sunlight to transform the water into oxygen. The carbon dioxide gains electrons, becoming glucose. The oxygen is then released back into the air.

Sessile

Sea creatures permanently attached to the seafloor, rock, or other firm base are called sessile. They cannot pursue food, nor run away from predators.

Submersible

A vehicle known as a submersible generally refers to one especially designed for deep-sea research.

Sunlight Zone

The sunlight zone is also known as the euphotic zone. It gets its name because this is the depth of the ocean where sunlight can still penetrate the water. It begins at the surface and continues to a depth of about 660 feet (~201 meters).

Tunic

In biology, a tunic is a layer or a sheath or a similar protective covering. It means about the same as a person wearing a kind of coat.

Twilight Zone

The twilight zone of the ocean is a layer of water beginning about 650 feet (200 meters) from the surface and extending down to about 3,300 feet (1,000 meters). It is also known as the mesopelagic or midwater zone. It is cold; the sun barely penetrates that far down. Studies show the amount of life in the twilight zone may be greater than all the rest of the ocean combined.

Venus Fly Trap

This is an insect-eating plant. Two hinged leaves snap shut on the bugs, trapping them for lunch.

Viscous

A thick, gooey substance, somewhere between a solid and a liquid.

Zooplankton

The word is a combination of two Greek words: 'zoo' refers to animals, and 'lanktos', which means 'wanderer' or 'drifter'. Zooplankton are usually microscopic; however, some (such as jellyfish and siphonophores) are larger.

Are You a Future Ocean Scientist?

Planning Your Future

Did this book spark your interest in possibly having a career researching what our oceans are all about? If so, here are some of the areas of study you want to consider at college. Also, you'll see resources listed where you might learn more before making a decision.

Areas of Study

- Applied Ocean Physics & Engineering
- Biogeochemistry
- Biological Oceanography
- Biology
- Geochemistry
- Geology & Geophysics
- Imaging
- Marine Chemistry & Geochemistry
- Marine Policy
- Mass Spectrometry
- Mathematical Ecology
- Micropaleontology
- Oceanographic Instrument Development and Support
- Physical Oceanography
- Underwater Vehicles (Autonomous, Tethered and Human-Occupied)

Resources to Learn More

- **Monterey Bay Aquarium Research Institute (MBARI)**
  This research institution began in 1985 with an HOV trip down deep in the waters off the coast of Central California. Frustrated by not being able to take videos of the magnificent animals, the diver, Bruce Robison, found an engineer who had made a quality camera possible to use at those depths. That camera let Robison inspire others to establish a full research program. Current research programs at MBARI include the entire ocean, from shallow water to the deep sea. The need to understand this 71 percent of our earth motivates all MBARI's research.

- **National Oceanic and Atmospheric Administration (NOAA)**
  Ocean Exploration Careers – Learn more about a variety of ocean careers available to those interested in work on or in the ocean.
  https://oceanexplorer.noaa.gov/edu/oceanage/welcome.html

- **Schmidt Ocean Institute**
  Schmidt Ocean Institute advances marine research around the world. It provides the most advanced operational and technological support, as well as acquiring and distributing information to aid such research.

- **Scripps Institution of Oceanography at UC San Diego**
  Scripps Institution of Oceanography at UC San Diego is the world leader in ocean and earth science research. It is also known for its dedication to educating the next generation of oceanographers. Oceanography is especially exciting because it requires experts from many different scientific and engineering fields. They feel it is one of the most exciting science careers imaginable. Preparing for a Career in Oceanography Booklet 2010 (ucsd.edu)

- ## University of Washington School of Oceanography

Excellent universities for the study of all fields of oceanography are located on both coasts (and some in between). The University of Washington School of Oceanography is located in Seattle, Washington. They offer a $40,000 annual award for research in ocean pollution and ocean change.
https://www.ocean.washington.edu/story/Paths_to_Becoming_an_Oceanographer

- ## Woods Hole Oceanographic Institution (WHOI)

K-12 students can learn more about Oceanography at the Woods Hole Oceanographic Institution (WHOI) website:
https://www.whoi.edu/know-your-ocean/ocean-topics/. WHOI offers coursework in ocean science and a semester-long research project advised by a WHOI scientist or engineer to undergraduate college students majoring in science, engineering or mathematics.

Recommended for Further Enjoyment and Learning

Books

- *Alien Deep* (National Geographic Kids) by Bradley Hague
- *Creatures of the Deep: In search of the Sea's Monsters and the World They Live In* by Erich Hoyt
- *Diving to a Deep-Sea Volcano* by Kenneth Mallory
- *Extreme Ocean* by Glen Phalen and Sylvia Earle
- *Leatherback Turtles, Giant Squids, and Other Mysterious Animals of the Deepest Seas* by Ana Maria Rodiguez
- *Sylvia Earle: Ocean Explorer* by Dennis Fertig

Videos

- Blobfish: Blobfish - Deepsea Oddities - YouTube https://www.youtube.com/watch?v=MobCeLyiM1Q
- Bloodybelly Comb Jelly: Bloodybelly comb jelly | Animals | Monterey Bay Aquarium https://www.montereybayaquarium.org/animals/animals-a-to-z/bloodybelly-comb-jelly
- Colossal Squid: The owner of this video is unknown. https://www.tepapa.govt.nz/discover-collections/read-watch-play/science/colossal-squid/life-and-habits-colossal-squid
- Cone Snail: NatGeo Wild The Deadly Cone Snail | World's Weirdest - YouTube https://www.youtube.com/watch?v=UwgZjEfBUS4
- Cone Snail: Watch These Cunning Snails Stab and Swallow Fish Whole | Deep Look - YouTube https://youtu.be/jYMjLgPFSso
- Medicines from the Sea: Medicines from the Sea | Ocean Today (noaa.gov) https://oceantoday.noaa.gov/medicinesfromthesea/
- Octopus: Octopus Steals Crab from Fisherman|Super Smart Animals|BBC Earth

- Real Life SpongeBob and Patrick—NOAA: https://oceanexplorer.noaa.gov/okeanos/explorations/ex2104/features/spongebob/media/58SecEX2104_VID_20210727T171000Z_ROV-640x360.mp4?640
- Submersible Alvin Reengineering: Reengineering an Iconic Sub to Explore Alien Worlds - YouTube https://www.youtube.com/watch?v=-QhLmOh6uAU
- Tardigrades (little water bears): Tardigrades Are the Toughest Animal on Earth that can Survive Space and Volcanoes | The Dodo - YouTube https://www.youtube.com/watch?v=IH3ABle9k7A
- Top 10 Sea Creatures: Monterey Bay Aquarium Research Institute https://www.youtube.com/watch?v=8oOG2BGrmyAYouTube

Other Fun Stuff

- **Take a quiz about underwater vehicles at the WHOI website**
  Underwater Vehicle Quiz (whoi.edu) https://divediscover.whoi.edu/underwater-vehicles/underwater-vehicle-quiz/
- **Take a quiz about Hydrothermal Vents at the WHOI website**
  Hydrothermal Vent Quiz (whoi.edu) https://divediscover.whoi.edu/hydrothermal-vents/vent-geology-chemistry-quiz/
- **Learn more about the ocean at the WHOI website**
  Know Your Ocean - Woods Hole Oceanographic Institution (whoi.edu) https://www.whoi.edu/know-your-ocean/
- **Pick your favorite ocean theme to learn more at the NOAA Ocean Exploration website**
  Education: Themes: NOAA Ocean Exploration https://oceanexplorer.noaa.gov/edu/themes/welcome.html

Diving Deeper

- Inspired by the Deep: A contest for students in grades 6–12. Become an inventor and learn about the wondrously strange creatures of the deep sea at the same time!
  Inspired By The Deep https://inspiredbythedeep.com/
- Follow a NOAA Ocean Exploration livestream NOAA Ocean Exploration Livestream: Camera 1 https://oceanexplorer.noaa.gov/livestreams/welcome.html#status
- Sea Grant Scholarship Opportunities: Sea Grant scholarships offer opportunities for financial assistance and research funding to students pursuing a career in STEM. Sea Grant > Students > Scholarships (noaa.gov) https://seagrant.noaa.gov/Students/Scholarships
- Deep-Sea Biology Society: External funding opportunities – DSBS (dsbsoc.org) https://dsbsoc.org/grants-awards/external-funding-opportunities/

Neither publisher nor author has any responsibility for the continuance or accuracy of URLs for external or third-party internet websites referred to in this book, nor is there any guarantee the content on said websites in whole or in part is, or will remain, accurate or appropriate.

Identity	Photo	Credit
Sloane's Viperfish		©Woods Hole Oceanographic Institution
Deep Sea Challenger		Jacques Dayan/Shutterstock
Alvin		©Woods Hole Oceanographic Institution
Ocean Depth Zones		VectorMine/Shutterstock
Shrimp Vomiting Light		Edith Widder, ORCA
Bioluminscent Deep Sea Lantern Fish		3dsam79/Shutterstock

Identity	Photo	Credit
Hydrothermal Vent		Pacific Ring of Fire 2004 Expedition. NOAA Office of Ocean Exploration; Dr. Bob Embley, NOAA PMEL, Chief Scientist.
Black Smokers		OAR/National Undersea Research Program (NURP); NOAA Photographer: P.Rona.
Blobfish		Copyright NORFANZ Founding Parties Photographer Kerryn Parkinson
Blobfish		NOAA OKEANOS Explorer Program, 2013 Northeast U. S. Canyons Expedition
Jellyfish		Eric Gilbert Creative/Shutterstock.com
Jellyfish bell shape		RLS Photo/Shutterstock.com

Identity	Photo	Credit
Jellyfish long tentacles		Archana Bhartia/Shutterstock
Bloodybelly comb jelly		Takokat/Shutterstock
Sea Squirt		©Woods Hole Oceanographic Institution
Giant Pacific Octopus		Photographer: Keith Morgan
Sloan's Viperfish		Woods Hole Oceanographic Institution
Anglerfish		Edith Widder, ORCA

Identity	Photo	Credit
Bristlemouth on Quarter		Woods Hole Oceanographic Institution
Grumpy Goosefish		Image courtesy of the NOAA Office of Ocean Exploration and Research, Gulf of Mexico 2018.
Colossal Squid		Illustration from SciePro/Shutterstock
Colossal Squid		Colossal squid, Mesonychoteuthis hamiltoni Robson, 1925, collected 2008, Ross Sea, Antarctica. Gift of the Ministry of Fisheries, 2007. CC BY 4.0. Te Papa (M.190318)
Pyrosome mouth		dlearyous photography/Shutterstock
Pyrosome colors		© Doug Perrine

Identity	Photo	Credit
Siphonophore		©Woods Hole Oceanographic Institution
Dandelion Siphonophore		Image courtesy of NOAA Office of Ocean Exploration and Research, Hohonu Moana 2016.
Tardigrade/ Water Bear		Dotted Yeti/Shutterstock
Tardigrade tun		Peddalanka Ramesh Babu/Shutterstock
Scuba Diver Collecting Sponge		timsimages.uk/Shutterstock
Mechanical Arm Collecting Sponge		Photo courtesy of Schmidt Ocean Institute

Identity	Photo	Credit
Cone Snail		Billy Watkins/Shutterstock
Jellyfish		Tereza Tothova/Shutterstock
Laura Bagge		
Eric Stackpole		
Eric Stackpole		

THE END